DISCOVERING
BEVERAGES

First published in 1992 by
Young Library Ltd
3 The Old Brushworks
56 Pickwick Road
Corsham, Wiltshire SN13 9BX
England

ISBN 1 85429 010 X

Printed in Hong Kong

Contents

written by
Liz Oram

designed and
illustrated by
Susannah Bradley

YOUNG LIBRARY

Tea

The dry, brown or black flakes in a packet of tea were once green leaves growing on beautiful hillsides.

The leaves are plucked from bushes by hand, usually by women. In India they are dressed in brightly coloured costumes called saris. They walk up and down the long slopes, between the rows of greenery, with large wicker baskets on their backs. They pluck just the top three or four leaves of each branch and toss them over their shoulders into the baskets.

What does the tea bush look like? It is a little shorter than you. It has dark green, shiny leaves and

white flowers. The tea bush grows best in warm, wet countries like India, China, Japan, Sri Lanka, Kenya, Malawi, and Bangladesh.

The leaves are dried, and machine-crushed between rollers. When the leaves are crushed the tea smell is released.

A tea picker at work in Kenya. He plucks only the top few leaves of each shoot, and tosses them into the basket on his back.

This is part of Europe's biggest teabag factory. Three weeks' production laid in a row would reach right round the world.

The crushed leaves are then placed in a warm, damp atmosphere for about four hours to FERMENT. The longer the tea is fermented, the stronger its flavour.

After fermentation the leaves are damp again, so hot air is blown through the tea to dry it. Finally, the tea is packed into large chests lined with foil or rice-paper.

A tea PLANTATION employs hundreds, or even thousands, of workers. Nearly all the people who live in tea-growing areas earn their living from it.

The tea chests are usually carried overseas in container ships. On arrival at the port the tea is taken to the tea auction. Buyers and sellers bargain with each other to get the prices they want.

As well as buyers and sellers, there are tea tasters. With a noisy slurp, they suck the tea from a large, round spoon. After rolling the tea over their tongue for a while, they spit it out! By tasting all the teas, they decide which are the best ones to buy.

Perhaps your family buys teabags. Or they might prefer 'loose' tea, which is sold in larger, airtight packets. It is spooned into a teapot, which has a grill over the spout to prevent any tea-leaves following the liquid into the cup.

Tea is a very easy drink to make – you simply

pour boiling water on to it, then leave it for a few minutes to 'brew'. In European countries most people add milk, and some add sugar. In the United States and Australia iced tea is very popular. In Tibet tea is squashed to form a solid block. They chip off bits of the block into cold water, boil the mixture (often for many hours) then add salt and a blob of butter! In Japan a host will sometimes honour his guests with an elaborate tea-serving ceremony which can last all afternoon!

Coffee

Perhaps you have tried coffee and decided you do not like its bitter flavour. However, adults enjoy coffee. All over the American continent, and in most European and Middle East countries, coffee is more popular than tea. In fact coffee is one of the world's biggest industries. If everyone stopped drinking coffee it would be a disaster for millions of

The picture above gives a helicopter view of a Columbian coffee plantation. The worker on the right is picking only the red cherries, leaving the green ones to ripen.

people. Most of them live in poorer, developing countries.

Coffee comes from a large, evergreen SHRUB called the coffee tree. It grows in Brazil, Mexico, Indonesia, Columbia, Kenya, Zaire, and many other TROPICAL countries. Like tea, it is grown on large plantations, containing thousands of trees. It can also be grown on much smaller farms run by a single family.

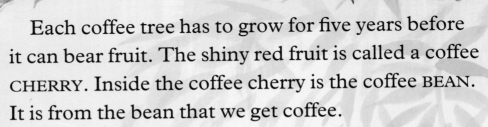

Each coffee tree has to grow for five years before it can bear fruit. The shiny red fruit is called a coffee CHERRY. Inside the coffee cherry is the coffee BEAN. It is from the bean that we get coffee.

The cherries have to be picked by hand because

they ripen at different times on the same branch. Each picker must take only the ripest cherries. They are spread out on the ground in the sun to dry for two or three weeks. Then they are split open and the coffee beans are removed. This is called 'hulling', and it is usually a machine that does it.

The green coffee beans are sent to the market where the coffee manufacturing companies buy

These Indonesian workers are enjoying a brief rest after a long day of picking the coffee cherries.

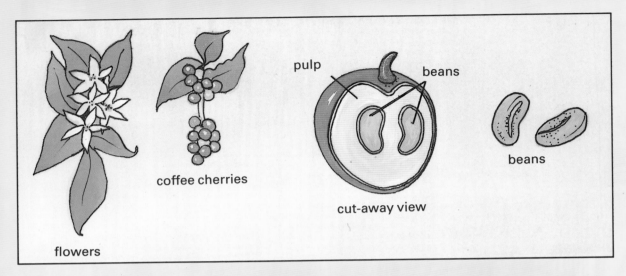

flowers

coffee cherries

pulp   beans

cut-away view

beans

them. They take their green beans to the factory, and roast them until they turn a lovely brown colour. Roasting develops the flavour of the coffee bean. Before it was sold, the coffee was tested by a taster. The taster took a sample from each farm, roasted it, and tasted the coffee made from it.

Coffee beans must be ground into a powder, so that they will give their flavour to the hot water. The size of the grains will depend on the way the

The freshly picked cherries are put through a pulping machine. It separates the pulp from the bean. Later the beans are spread in the sun to dry.

coffee is to be used. For filter machines it will be ground very finely. For percolators the grains will be larger.

Most coffee is sold already ground. You can also buy the beans and grind them yourself just before making the coffee – it tastes better that way, but is more trouble. The least trouble of all is instant coffee. This is ground so finely that it dissolves in a cup of boiling water and is ready to drink immediately. Ground coffee is packed airtight, for it

The countries which grow most tea, coffee, and cocoa

Tea
1 India
2 China
3 Sri Lanka
4 Georgia
5 Azerbaijan
6 Kenya
7 Turkey
8 Indonesia

Coffee
1 India
6 Kenya
8 Indonesia
9 Brazil
10 Columbia
11 Mexico
12 Ivory Coast
13 Ethiopia

Cocoa
9 Brazil
12 Ivory Coast
14 Malaysia
15 Ghana
16 Nigeria
17 Cameroon
18 Ecuador

Tropic of Cancer

Tea

Coffee

Cocoa

Tea and Coffee

Coffee and Cocoa

Equator

Tropic of Capricorn

13

goes stale if exposed to the air.

The French make coffee with hot milk and serve it in large bowls at breakfast. They dip their breads and pastries into it. Middle Easterners drink a very strong type of coffee called Turkish coffee, served in tiny cups, and sipped between swallows of water. Some people like iced coffee, which is chilled and sipped from tall glasses. There are several ways of enjoying coffee, but you probably prefer the drink in the next chapter.

Cocoa

Like coffee, cocoa comes from a tree which grows in the tropics. About half the world's cocoa grows in the West African countries of Ghana, Ivory Coast, Nigeria, and Cameroon. Most of the rest comes from Central and South America – Mexico, Brazil, San Domingo, and Ecuador – and Malaysia.

What is this tree called? It is the CACAO tree. Cacao is a Spanish word; and our word 'cocoa' is a different form of it. You just have to remember that the cocoa drink comes from the cacao tree.

The fruits of the cacao tree grow straight out of the trunk and main branches. This Ghanaian boy is chopping off only the golden-yellow ones. The green ones are not ripe yet.

After the pods are chopped from the trees, the workers hack them open to remove the beans.

Like the tea bush and the coffee tree, cacao trees grow best in plantations. However, there are also much smaller family-sized farms.

The fruit of the cacao tree is called a POD. When fully grown it is about the size and shape of an American football. It does not hang from the branches but grows directly from the trunk.

Each pod contains about forty seeds, called 'beans'. They are gleaming white and covered in a

16

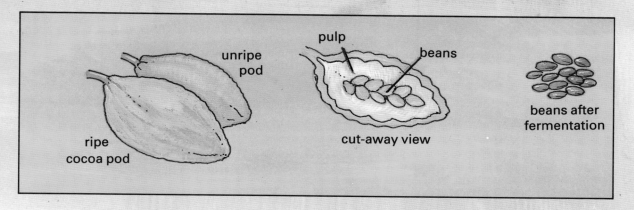

unripe
pod

ripe
cocoa pod

pulp

beans

cut-away view

beans after
fermentation

slimy pulp. Yet cocoa powder is a chocolate-brown
colour. How are the white cacao beans turned into
dark brown cocoa powder?

The workers know when a pod is ready to be
picked, for it ripens from green to yellow. They cut
the pods off the tree with a very sharp knife, put
them into an enormous heap, then sit round it all
day splitting the pods open. The small, white, cacao

beans can be seen lying in neat rows.

Now, the beans have to be removed from the
pods. This is no one's favourite job! People work for
hours in the hot sun, scraping the slimy beans out of
the pod with wooden spatulas, and flicking them
into baskets. It is very hot and sticky work.

The next job is to ferment the beans, to develop

17

their flavour. The workers lay a few banana leaves on the ground, pile the beans on top, then cover the heap with more leaves. The pile of beans get damp and hot. After five or six days the beans are beginning to darken. They are spread out in the sun to dry for several more days. Then they are packed

The beans are fermented, then spread out on mats to dry for several days. Then they are ready to be sold.

into bags, and sold (usually to the government). The government sells the cocoa beans to companies overseas.

At last it is time to turn these RAW COCOA beans into cocoa. At first they are roasted, to a red-brown colour, then pressed into a block. The yellow, greasy liquid which oozes out is called COCOA BUTTER. The pressed beans are then ground into a fine powder. This is the cocoa which you see in tins and packets in the supermarket. If you're lucky you get a delicious drink of it before you go to bed.

COCOA POWDER is not only used to make drinks. It is often used to flavour cakes, biscuits, and sweets. It is a pity there is not enough space here to tell you about another use – chocolate. Chocolate is made from a mixture of cocoa powder and cocoa butter. Life wouldn't be the same without chocolate, would it?

Soft Drinks

It is possible that some of you have never drunk tea, or coffee, or cocoa. But every reader of this book has enjoyed a soft drink. Soft drinks are fruit juices, or mixtures of fruit juice and water. Lemonade, orange squash, cola, ginger beer, blackcurrant juice – can you think of any more?

Most soft drinks are fizzy because they are made partly of carbonated water. Carbonated water contains a gas called carbon dioxide. The fizzing sound when you open a can or bottle of lemonade is the noise of some of the carbon dioxide gas escaping. If you leave the top off the bottle for a long while, the drink loses its fizz. All the gas has escaped. So always screw the top tightly back on if

Here are some of the delicious fruits which are used in soft drinks. How many do you recognize?

you don't want the drink to go flat.

There are three main types of soft drink. The first is fruit juice – the juice which runs out of fruit when it is crushed. The most popular fruits are orange, pineapple, apple, and grapefruit. Fruit juices are very good for you, but they don't quench your thirst much.

The second type is concentrated fruit juice – fruit juice with the natural water content taken out at the

factory. You wouldn't drink it like that. You pour only a small amount into the glass, then top it up with water from the tap. Orange, lemon, and blackcurrant are some of the favourite concentrated drinks. They are often called squash – orange squash, lemon squash, and so on.

The third type of soft drink is the fizzy one. Fizzy drinks are concentrated fruit juice with carbonated water added. The best known fizzy drink is Coca-

cola. Two other favourites are lemonade and ginger beer.

Most soft drinks also have added flavourings and colourings. Some flavourings come from plants – from fruits, berries, or herbs.

Most soft drinks except pure fruit juice have added sugar. Sugar is very sticky stuff. It clings to your teeth and breaks down the protective covering. Therefore, after enjoying your orange squash or Coke, it is a good idea to brush your teeth.

22

Glossary

bean: The seed of the coffee and cacao trees.

brewing: Preparing a drink of tea by soaking the leaves in almost boiling water.

cacao: The tree from which we obtain cocoa.

carbonated water: Water which has had carbon dioxide added, to make it fizzy.

cherry: The fruit of the coffee tree, which contains the coffee bean.

cocoa butter: The liquid fat which runs out of cocoa beans when they are crushed.

cocoa powder: Ground and roasted cocoa beans, used in making chocolate, cake flavourings, and drinks.

fermentation: A chemical change causing partial decay. Tea leaves are fermented by leaving them in a warm, damp atmosphere.

plantation: A large area of land under cultivation, usually of only one crop. Usually all its workers live on the site.

pod: The fruit of the cacao tree, which contains the cocoa beans.

raw cocoa: Cocoa before it has been roasted and ground.

shrub: A short, woody plant with several stems.

tropical: In the area of the tropics. The tropics are marked on the map on pages 12 and 13.

Photo Sources
Allied-Lyons: page 4
Cadbury-Schweppes: page 18 (left), cover and page 1 (bottom left).
Environmental Picture Library: page 3.
Image Bank, London: page 21.
Imperial Chemical Industries: page 18 (right).
International Coffee Organisation: pages 7 (both), 9, 11 (both), and cover (middle right).
Rowntree-Mackintosh: pages 15, 16.
Tea Council, London: cover and page 1 (top right).

Index

Artwork

Among the subjects illustrated are Indian tea-pickers, pages 2/3; tea-packing, page 4; Japanese tea ceremony, page 6; coffee cherry-pickers in West Africa, pages 8/9; coffee-tasting, page 11; a pod-bearing cacao tree, page 15; Ghanaian workers removing beans from cocoa pods and drying them in the sun, pages 18/19.